GBS

Jason Hall

GBS

OBERON BOOKS
LONDON

First published in 2006 by Oberon Books Ltd
521 Caledonian Road, London N7 9RH
Tel: 020 7607 3637 / Fax: 020 7607 3629
e-mail: info@oberonbooks.com
www.oberonbooks.com

A catalogue record for this book is available from the British Library.

Cover design by James Jary Design

ISBN: 1 84002 702 9 / 978-1-84002-702-0

Printed in Great Britain by Antony Rowe Ltd, Chippenham

For Mr & Mrs W E Hall

Characters

RICH is early thirties, heavy set, with a goatee.

SAM is slightly younger and slimmer.

They are brothers.

Notes

Time The present

Place The suburbs of Toronto

Staging The play uses a combination of direct audience address and conventional dialogue. In addition to this, the actors are also required to play or provide the voices for other characters. The text suggests how the direct address may be handled and how the other voices may be divided between the actors. Ultimately, however, the company is given a certain degree of flexibility to decide how best to represent both these features in production.

Interval If the production requires an interval, it should occur between Scenes 14 and 15.

GBS was first performed on 30 June 2004 at the Factory Studio Theatre, Toronto, as part of the Toronto International Fringe Theatre Festival, where it won the Patron's Pick Award. The company were:

RICH, Daniel Dumsha

SAM, Stephen Sheffer

Director Megan McCoy

Assistant Director Phil Connell

Stage Manager Michael Hodgson

Produced by DeCo. Productions

GBS received its European premiere in this revised version on 23 November 2006 at Theatre 503, London, with the following company:

RICH, Kristian Brunn

SAM, Daniel Fine

Director Anna Ledwich

Designer Helen Goddard

Lighting Designer Phil Hewitt

Assistant Director Katharine Monaghan

Creative Producer Andrew Fishwick

Assistant Producer Kate Mackonochie

Prologue

Lights up on RICH and SAM.

RICH   Numbers.

SAM   Letters.

RICH   There are so many numbers. That's all I can think.

SAM   I listen to him begin, saying those letters.

RICH   I sit there in the kitchen, and I look at the book.

SAM   And every acronym I can think of starts rushing through my head.

RICH   I look at the book, because I sure don't know it by heart, and I think, look at all those numbers.

SAM   How many acronyms can you think of?

RICH   I don't think, what am I going to say, or how is he going to react. I just think, look at all those fucking numbers.

SAM   But the thing with an acronym, unless it's unique, one of a kind, it tells you nothing.

RICH   It makes you not want to dial, there are so many.

SAM   Unless it's unique, it's just letters.

RICH   There are too many numbers.

1

RICH   G. B. S. The doctor said. Really slow. Like I'm some kind of idiot. And I wanted to say, I know the fucking alphabet you asshole. I know the letters G, B, and S. What do they stand for? What do they mean? I say that last bit. I tell him. What does it mean, I say, this GBS? Guillain-Barré Syndrome, he says. Still all slow. And then he folds his hands, gets all serious, and leans back. He sits there.

Well, that clears it up, doesn't it? Gee-um-bar-eh syndrome. As if that means anything to me. But he's not offering anything up and I can see that I'm going to have to ask again. He wants me to ask again. A part of me just wants to go, oh yeah right, GBS, thought so, and get up and leave. Asshole doctor. But Mom is right there and I know she wants to ask but can't ask, can't talk, can't do anything and has, quite frankly, been a mess the last two days, so it's up to me. So I ask.

Clearly it's what he's been waiting for. Out come the brochures, and he's talking about percentages, and treatments, and then, and this really pisses me off, he looks right at me and says, You said you were a mechanic, right? And I can tell what's coming next. It's right there in his voice. Before he even does it, I know he's going to make some comparison to fixing a car or something else, you know, manual, like I'm some peasant manual labourer, he's going to compare it to that, so someone stupid like me can understand. And that's exactly what he does. Think of the nervous system as the body's electrical wiring, he says. So I sit there, gritting my teeth and I really just want to pop him one, right between the eyes, right in the middle of his little explanation, just more than anything for the shock and the surprise. And to make me feel better. Because I know it would.

But then he's finished and the next thing I know Mom is thanking him and, this I cannot believe, giving him a hug and sobbing into his white doctor's jacket. And he's looking over the top of her head at me with one of those 'can you please take her off me?' looks. Which pisses me off even more. So I peel her away and force a thanks at him through my teeth.

In the hall I tell her we should head home but no way, she wants to stay by his side, but for God's sake she's still wearing that purple velour tracksuit she threw on Sunday night. And on her feet? Flip-flops. Two days she's been dressed like this. Looks like a bag lady. Come on, I tell her. We can be back in a couple of hours. Just go home, get changed, have a bath, and we'll be right back. Grudgingly, she goes for it.

Well, as soon as we're in the parking lot, not even off hospital property yet, I'm wishing I'd kept my mouth shut, and just left her there.

Did you call Sam yet?

Did I call Sam yet. Of course I have not called Sam, I haven't even thought about calling Sam. I tell her no.

He really needs to know, says Mom. What that means, by the way, is *I* need to tell him. No, actually what that really means is I should have already told him. When we first got to the hospital and she was in that panic and kept saying what about Sam, what about Sam? That meant I was supposed to deal with it. Like I didn't have other things on my mind, like Sam makes one bit of difference to me.

I'll call him, I say. And as I say it, I hit the gas so hard pulling out of the hospital, the tyres screech, and Mom goes, Easy dear! I apologise. But I don't really mean it. Almost makes up for not smacking the doctor.

We get out onto Markham Road and with the sight of everyday stuff, people and cars, and gas stations, and doughnut shops, with all that, the real world starts flooding back in around me. I've got things to do, I'm a busy man. Need to eat something, I'm fucking starving. Need to call work, let 'em know I need another day or two, that's gonna go down well. Need to call Beth and make sure she got Julia to school today. What I *don't* need is another call from the secretary asking, is Julia coming in today? Damn near gave me a heart attack. Had to get straight on the phone to Beth, right there in the hospital hallway, why the hell isn't she at school? Oh, she says, I thought it would be fun for us to hang out together, since we only ever have weekends. Little bit of accusation there in her voice. Little bit of smugness too. Well. Yelled so loud, got shushed by two separate nurses. Sir, when patients are trying to sleep, we do not shout the word bitch in this hospital. I guess when they're awake it's okay? Nurse bitch.

Julia better be at school today, I'll tell you that much. Think I better call Beth first, then work…

By the time we get back home, I've got a hundred things on my mind. I can feel my shoulders clenching and I need that release, but no time for the bag, I head straight for the phone.

As soon as I pick it up Mom's waving her arms, wait wait wait, and she's shoving this blue book in my face.

He should be in now, she says, he's got Tuesdays and Wednesdays off. At first I have no idea what the hell she's talking about. Then I think she's talking about Dad, and for a second I think she's lost it, having delusions, which is all I need. Then I realise. Sam. She wants me to call Sam.

I take the book from her. She points to the spot on the page, then says she's going for a quick bath. She'll talk to him after, Sam and I could use the time to catch up. Then she's gone. I'm left standing in the kitchen. I'm standing here on my own.

I look down at the writing.

Sam. Cellphone. London.

He says the numbers slowly, considering each one.

011 44 7962 881765.

And all I can think is, there are so many numbers. It makes you not want to dial. There are too many numbers.

2

SAM   He's gotten so fucking fat it's tragic. Honestly. I come out of the gate and I'm looking for my brother but instead I find some blob. Still recognisable as him, but...God, he's taking this *heavy*weight thing too far. I mean, former features are still there, I can still tell it's him, but like sadder, and more serious, like he's trapped inside a fatter person and just can't get out. *Fat.* It's the only word. With a goatee. Which I do not understand at all, I mean fatness *and* facial hair? Aren't they the lethal F-s that no one should have, along with floral prints, fake tan, and Fred Perry? Not that they know who Fred Perry is here. I mean.

Oh! The best? So I finally realise that the mound of flesh is actually Rich, and I wave and kind of hustle over to him. And what does he come out with to greet me? The first words for our big, you know, reunion or reconciliation or whatever it is that we're having at this moment? What does he say?

RICH   Still skinny as ever, huh?

SAM   And I am like…well, first of all, I'm like fuck off you fat bastard, what are you, jealous? But then I'm like, bite your tongue, this is not about the two of you. It's about Dad. And Mom.

So I just grin tightly, and say, yep!

Anyway, he grunts something about the meter and how expensive the parking is and we're running, literally, to the car park. And I'm like, hello, I was just in transit for nine hours, okay? I am jet-lagged, and stressed, and upset at all of this and I haven't been home in, God I don't know, like three years and here I am, *sprinting* so we can save a dollar on parking. I'm as skinny as ever? He's as cheap as ever, possibly worse. I mean, sure, his situation, I understand it's tough. But clearly the money he saves isn't going to Julia. It's going to Taco Bell.

So we get to the car – very nice, I'll give him that, quite sporty, no idea what the hell it is, but nice – but we get stuck behind another car in the queue, and don't make it out in time, he has to pay that dollar. Sorry, *I* have to pay that dollar since, you know, we *have* to split the parking.

Anyway, whatever, it's like 40p. So we pull out and, get this, he screeches the fucking tyres. I mean, as if he still does that. Grow up. I'm sorry if I've put you out, but how the hell else am I supposed to get home from the airport? The subway really needs to come out here. Honestly.

I take out my Benson & Hedges, but before I can even get the plastic off, Rich is like:

RICH   Don't even think about smoking in my car.

SAM   And I'm like, sorry. Meanwhile, I'm absolutely dying for one, but hey, since when have my needs ever been a consideration?

        We drive in silence. After a few minutes I can tell if I want any answers I'm going to have to ask, because he's not offering anything up or, got forbid, asking anything about me. Would it kill him to show a bit of interest? But no, he never wanted me around and it looks like he hasn't changed.

        So I ask, What are the doctors saying now?

RICH   Same.

SAM   Kinda grunts it. It's this GBS then?

        He takes this deep breath, like it's the last thing he wants to talk about.

RICH   Well…it doesn't fit the classic example of what GBS symptoms are, so they're not sure.

SAM   And then he's giving me this, like, medical lecture on GBS, explaining to me what it is and it's exactly the same thing, like word for word exactly the same thing he said on the phone when he called me on Tuesday.

RICH   Think of the body's nervous system like the electrical
        wiring in a house,

SAM   He says. The electrical wiring in a house? Like he hasn't
        already told me this. Like I don't already know this. Like
        I haven't scoured the internet for information. Like I
        haven't grilled that Liam, the one we hired to work in the
        middle bar, nursing student, nice kid, to see if he knew
        anything about it at all. Whatever. I let Rich explain. I'm
        sure it makes him feel smart.

        But I hate the way he keeps saying it. Gee-um-bar-eh
        syndrome. He so obviously studied the phonetic spelling.
        And he still can't get it right.

        When he told me on the phone, he was too embarrassed
        to say it at first, Guillain-Barré. So he called it GBS. And
        I remember him saying it the very first time, very slowly,
        The doctor thinks what's causing the coma is GB... And
        at that moment every acronym I could think of went
        flying through my head. I mean, how many acronyms
        can you think of? Hundreds? Thousands? Well, don't
        laugh, but for a second I thought the next thing he was
        going to say was L, I honestly did. GBL. You know,
        gamma butyrolactone? Clubbing drug, we get more and
        more of those idiots in with each passing week, G written
        on their hands in case they take too much. I mean, the
        thought of Dad on *that*, G on his hand? It's just...no.
        Then I thought what if it's not GBL but GBH, grievous
        bodily harm, and was suddenly terrified, maybe someone
        attacked him, split his head open? Then Rich comes out
        with the S. GBS. And what's my next thought?

        George Bernard Shaw. The playwright. I mean, what, he
        was paralysed by *Pygmalion*? He wouldn't be the first...

Rich is turning off the motorway. We're not going home?
I say.

RICH   Nope,

SAM   He says.

Please tell me you're not taking me to the hospital, I
say. I need a cup of coffee first. A rest would be great, a
shower would be heaven, but I'll settle for a coffee. That's
all I ask.

RICH   We're not going to the hospital.

SAM   So where are we going?

Silence. And it's the kind of silence which means stay
silent.

I see we're in the deepest darkest suburbs now. I see
we're still graced by the sign that says: 'Prepare yourself
– Jesus is coming!' Since that fucking thing has been up
for about twenty years, JC doesn't seem to be in any rush.
And really, if there's anywhere that could use a visit from
him, it's here. What an urban planning nightmare. All the
necessary parts of a city, but everything in completely the
wrong places, completely the wrong combinations. Kind
of like a good meal, after you've just thrown it up.

Rich is pulling into a parking lot in front of some
apartments. Not condos, mind you. Apartments. With
youths out front that look, well, I hate to say it, but if the
shoe fits, well, they rather look like hoodlums. They've
got *bikes*. You know, *baseball* hats? And they're staring at
us.

The car door opens up and Rich says:

RICH   Back in a sec.

SAM   And the door slams. I look at the hoodlums. I mean, I
        feel safe here.

3

RICH   Go fuck myself? *Go fuck myself?* This is the thanks I get,
        this is the appreciation for all her shit I put up with, for
        showing some concern about my daughter? Go fuck
        myself? I don't think so. She can go fuck *her*self.

        I walk up to the lobby and, shit, forgot about the buzzer,
        she's gonna have to buzz me up, but she's not gonna do
        that, no way. Shit. I stand there feeling kind of stumped.
        Look back at the car, as if that's gonna help.

        Sam. Fucking Sam. Look at him, staring at those
        kids, totally shitting himself. Don't they have gangs in
        London? Look at him. Terrified. Good.

        Then I think, hang on a second.

        I walk back out to the car and wave him over. I can see
        him not getting it.

SAM   (What the hell is he…?)

RICH   Get the fuck over here, I yell. He gets it now, scrambles
        out of the car, and comes up, looking all pissed off.

SAM   What?

RICH   I need you to do something.

SAM   Like what?

RICH   Go up to the intercom there.

SAM   Yeah.

RICH   And press 0811.

SAM   Yeah.

RICH   It's Beth's place.

SAM   Oh.

RICH   When she picks up, tell her it's you. You just got into town and want to see Julia 'cause you haven't seen her in ages.

SAM   I *haven't* seen her in ages.

RICH   Well there you go.

SAM   Why can't you buzz up?

RICH   Never mind that.

SAM   Because I don't want to get caught up in some custody, you know, thing. It's not my place.

RICH   It's not his place. This guy…

        Just buzz the intercom, will you?

SAM   Is this legal? Do you have some kind of restraining –

RICH   Just buzz the fucking intercom!

SAM   All right! Fucking hell, stop yelling at me! Jesus.

RICH   So finally he punches in the numbers. And we hear the ringing. And then, her voice.

        Hello? she says.

        And he's looking all confused.

        RICH gestures with his hands for SAM to say something. He does this throughout the following whenever SAM seems to be at a loss for words.

SAM   Um… Beth?

RICH   And she goes, Yeah?

SAM   Beth this is Sam. (*Pause.*) Rich's brother Sam. (*Pause.*) Julia's uncle? (*Pause.*) Living in England?

RICH   Then she gets it, and is suddenly all like, Jesus Christ Sam, oh my God, is that really you?

SAM   Um, yeah.

RICH   And she's like, How the hell are you and I'm so sorry about your Dad, and blah blah blah, and the two of them are getting right into a nice little catch-up session, right in the lobby. So I give him a smack to remind him what the hell we're doing here.

SAM   Ouch!

RICH   He says. Pussy.

SAM   Sorry about that, Beth, no I'm fine. (Asshole.) Um, look, the reason I came by is I was wondering if I could see Julia. Since I'm in town.

RICH   There's a slight pause on her end, and I'm beginning to think she's figured it out. But then she goes, Oh Sam, I'm really sorry, she's at one of her friends' place.

        Sam goes:

SAM   Oh.

RICH   I think: fuck.

        But, then she's inviting him up anyway and says maybe she can get Julia back early. Maybe? *Maybe?* She's only her mother, she better damn well be able to get her back early.

Anyway, she buzzes us in, and we walk down the hallway
that stinks of curry, get in the elevator, which also stinks
of curry, and go up to the eighth floor which actually
doesn't smell of curry, which is a shame, 'cause instead it
smells like feet.

I hate this place. I hate that Julia has to spend her
weekends here. It makes my shoulders go tense.

We get to the door and he just stands there.

What?

SAM   I have to knock?

RICH   Yes you have to knock.

SAM   Why?

RICH   The peephole. Idiot. The *peephole.* He gets this look on his
face.

SAM   What's going on here, Rich?

RICH   I'm just about to smack him again when I hear chains
rattle on the other side of the door. The locks clunking.
Her voice saying Sam, is that you? And then it swings
open. It swings wide open.

4

SAM   It's not a punch. I wouldn't it call it that. Not a punch,
no. That conjures the wrong image. You hear punch you
think close-fisted. You think, yes, probably, a closed fist
in someone's face, maybe a nose breaking, teeth being
spit out. Crude and blunt and ugly. That's not what this
is. But it's not a slap either. Certainly not. Not that open-

handed, sharp, short, incredibly loud thing that a slap is. A slap is this spontaneous eruption, this emotional thing, unexpected and unplanned, I think, by both people involved. It comes from nowhere. That's not what this is. This comes from somewhere.

Not a slap. Not a punch. What is it? What would you call it? It's surgical. Automatic. And strangely beautiful.

Whatever that first thing was when Rich and Beth saw each other, that thing after the moment, that half second where they just stared at each other, whether it was a slap or something else, the end result is the same.

Beth kicked the living shit out of Rich. Seriously.

First this kind of *phoom* with her hand, then this *bap* with the other, and I hear her foot go *thump* on his, and then there's a *foof* as he goes flying, head over heels into her apartment, and lands flat on his back. Hard. And he's gasping for breath and wincing in pain, I mean his back is probably fucking broken, but she's in there as quick as she can, merciless by the look of it, straddling his chest and doing some kind of arm thing across his neck. His eyes are bulging.

I should've known, she's yelling, You fucking asshole, I should've known you would try something like this. What did I tell you? What did I tell you? I have her on weekends and I don't care if I did have her a few days extra this week, that doesn't change the arrangement! If she needs to see her grandpa, I'll bring her. Okay? You hear me? Are you listening now you stubborn fuckwad? Can you hear me?

Rich makes this gurgle which, I guess, could be interpreted as a yes.

RICH   (*Gurgles.*)

SAM   I suddenly realise that I'm just standing there, watching the whole thing like it's a film. Maybe I should do something, like, help somehow. Beth clearly has the same thought at the same time. So she glares. At me.

I'm terrified. What if I'm next?

Instead she just says: How was the flight? Which, it has to be said, is a higher level of interest than I got from the 'stubborn fuckwad' on the floor there.

Turbulent, I say. Surprisingly good food, though.

I hear they've made a lot of advancements in the quality of air catering, she says.

The quantities have definitely improved, I say. But the coffee is still crap.

Rich gurgles again.

RICH   (*Gurgles.*)

SAM   Beth smiles a little. You still smoke, she asks?

And I, without even a second thought, fix my eyes on the Craven A she's holding out…and to get at it, I step right over Rich.

5

RICH   Okay, sure, Julia mentioned her mother was taking classes. Classes. And, yes, okay, maybe she mentioned the words ju-jitsu in there, but, really, what the fuck do I care what Beth is up to? I purposely try and *filter out* any information about Beth's life that doesn't directly impact on me or my daughter.

What the hell did she think I was going to do? Did I ever, once, raise a hand to her when we were together? In all those years? Did I ever threaten to hurt her? No way. Absolutely not. If I got upset, I'd always go downstairs, work out on the bag. In my head? Think about hitting some guy in the ring, usually that asshole down at the club, never think about her. Never even imagine it.

I mean, ju-jitsu classes. Who takes ju-jitsu?

6

SAM   In my opinion they were a match made in Hell from the beginning. Sure, Rich can be a cocky thick-headed asshole sometimes – most of the time. But Beth…Beth was never the most, shall we say, tactful person either. Like the time she told us about being 'on the rag' during thanksgiving dinner. Or her colourful vocabulary when describing ethnic minorities – my favourite was the way she used to refer to our neighbours, the Husseins, as 'sand niggers'. Or her opinion that 'brown people' can't drive. I won't even tell you what 'jo-jos' are. So, I hope Rich appreciates the fact I'm attempting to diffuse this situation by smoking the peace pipe with his lovely ex-wife.

I look at Beth. I'm hoping we can continue to exchange pleasantries until Rich is capable of standing up again. Wrong. As I'm handing her back her Casino Rama lighter, she goes, So. Heard you got fired from the BBC.

I wasn't fired, I say, casual as I can be. My contract ended.

Oh right, she says, before slipping in: They didn't renew it though did they.

I mean this is not news, okay? She knows all this. This is like a few years ago.

No, I say. They did not renew it.

Shame, she says. We all thought you were gonna make it big over there. All that experience you had with the CBC. Guess that didn't pay off in the end.

No, I say.

Ah well, she says. Life is a highway.

What…the *fuck* does that mean? I just say, Yes, and grit my teeth. And then I find myself like justifying the whole reason why the Beebs didn't renew with me. I'm going on about cutbacks, and the fact it's difficult to get work when you're not British, and how there were no contracts going for the kind of work I'm strong on, and all the while as my mouth is running on I'm thinking hang on here: why am I explaining myself to my – what is she – ex-sister-in-law?

She cuts me off. But you like what you're doing now, right? You're working in a bar?

Yes, I say.

You like that? she says.

Yes, I say.

You like working in a bar? she says.

Yes, I say. Again.

That's great, she says. And then, and I know it's coming, she asks, What's the bar called again?

I mean I get asked this question all the time, you know? Why don't I just have a standard response, a lie? Why can't I just say it's The Frog and Fiddler or The Dog and Duchess or some random name like that? But no. Not me. I have to say the truth:

It's called COK.

She laughs a little. It's called cock?

No, I say, getting a bit annoyed here. C. O. K.

And what does that stand for, she says?

'Carry On Klubbing'. She laughs.

And I know 'clubbing' is spelt with a C, I say.

Whatever, she says, still chuckling to herself. And thankfully, what follows is a silence just long enough for me to finish the fag, and stuff it down the neck of a nearby bottle of 50.

COK. Why do I always have to be so honest?

7

RICH   I can't believe he still smokes. I remember when he started back in high school. I saw him, out by the parking lot where everyone goes. And I was like, What the fuck are you doing? And he was like:

SAM   Stop pretending to be Dad.

RICH   And I was like, Yeah well maybe you'd prefer it if I told him then *he* can tell you to stop. Well. That freaked him out. For weeks after it was like: You won't tell him will you? 'Cause he knew if Dad found out it would be ugly.

See, Dad was one of those guys who had the whole 'if I ever catch you smoking I'm going to sit you down and make you smoke a whole pack' thing going on. The difference with Dad is, you kinda believed him. Because, apparently, that's what his Dad did to him. And Dad could go into some serious detail about what smoking a whole pack of cigarettes at once does to you. You can imagine why Sam was freaked. So for weeks I had this amazing piece of blackmail, which was great. Got to use the car when I wanted, got to watch my shows on TV, didn't have to clean up the dog shit. Was good. And of course I was never gonna tell Dad 'cause, you know, it's just not what you do, but the threat of it…well, scared the shit out of Sam. But in the end I never had to tell Dad. Sam fucked it up all by himself.

See, I don't know what he was doing, was at some party or something and for God knows what reason he was wearing a candy bracelet on his wrist. You know the kind? Little candy loops they string an elastic through? Julia's crazy about them. Don't ask me why the Hell he was wearing it at like seventeen, I don't even want to hazard a guess. Anyway, at one point in the evening he goes to take a bite off the bracelet but doesn't realise he's also holding a cigarette in the same hand. Whatever way he bends his head down to take a bite of the bracelet, the lit end of the cigarette goes right up his nose. Like, right up. As soon as he feels the burning, he goes to yank the thing out. Natural reaction. But the problem is he also takes a sharp inhale of breath 'cause he's so surprised by the pain. And he inhales so hard, that he sucks the lit end up off the tip of the cigarette and all the way up into his sinuses. Fucking idiot.

Next thing I know is we're getting a call at home, sitting in front of the TV with Mom and Dad, and it's the hospital. We rush over in a panic but when we find out what happened, well, I mean sure there's relief at first and then I almost piss myself laughing. Mom is relieved. And Dad? Dad is just pissed off.

This guy. Okay, I appreciate what he's doing here with Beth, giving me a bit of time to try and catch my breath, but come on. How he can even touch a cigarette now is beyond me. See, when Sam got out of the hospital the day after the little cigarette-inhaling accident, his nose all bandaged up and everything tasting like sawdust, Dad picked him up and drove him home. But on the way, they made a little stop off in Thompson Park. Dad took him to a picnic table, sat him down, and gently placed a plastic Bic lighter in front of him. Then after a few moments, what did he do? Dad slapped down a large pack of smokes. And he waited.

But, hey. I guess some people never change. (*He tries to move and grimaces in pain.*) Ow!

8

SAM   He won't let me drive. He can barely walk, but oh no, God forbid, he should let anyone else behind the wheel of his precious whatever it is. I might 'forget which side of the road to drive on'. As if living in London has erased my fucking memory. I mean. Oh, the hoodlums, by the

way, find it hilarious when we stagger out to the car. Me
trying to support Rich's fat ass. It takes forever. But, hey,
he can drive. He'll be fine.

When we pull out of the car park, I notice this time the
tyres don't screech.

I want to have a rest. Or a cup of coffee. But what
am I going to say? The silence is there again. The
impenetrable one. I don't know what to do, where to put
my eyes. I look out the window.

Has a city ever had so many doughnut shops?

And I think, with mild horror, that I've probably been in
most of them, and, yes, in fact most of these on, where
are we now? Ellesmere. Of course. Ellesmere Road. I've
certainly been in most of them, what else is there to do
when you're a teenager in the suburbs? You tour the
doughnut shops. Learn to smoke. Learn to drink coffee.

Rich turns down Bellamy, and the sprawling fields
unfold on either side of the road like upturned hands.
Hydrofields. Why is it no other place in the world
seems to have these, these gigantic scars cutting across
the face of the city, these scars stitched up with cables?
Hydrofields. At least it's somewhere to walk the dog. And
under the metal giants it's somewhere you can learn to
drink. Where you can learn to smoke weed. Where you
can find some porn in the bushes. Hydrofields.

Scarberia. The scars of the suburbs. Suburbia. *Sub*-urban.
Even the word sounds inferior. How did I ever live here?

(*Looks at RICH.*) How does he still live here?

And as if to answer me, he starts slowing down. This
serious look on his face. I haven't seen him look like this

in ages. Not ever. That look, it's…concern. Worry. Not like he's in pain, no, not physical pain. Something deeper. And then I think, what if he's breaking down? What if the stress of it all is finally, you know, grinding him down to, well, this. He doesn't look good. Jesus, I hope he doesn't start crying on me.

But then again, it would be an improvement on all the yelling he's been doing.

9

RICH THOSE FUCKING LITTLE ASSHOLES, I SWEAR TO GOD I WILL GET BACK TO THEIR SHITTY LITTLE APARTMENT, FIND EACH ONE OF THEM AND CAVE IN THEIR SKULLS WITH A CROWBAR! MY CAR, MY FUCKING CAR! LITTLE COCKSUCKING BASTARD SHITHEAD MOTHERFUCKING CUNTFACED PRICKS! COWARDLY LITTLE FUCKING SHITS!

I get out of the car and slam the door. Hard. The whole thing shakes but I couldn't care less. I look back and, yep, there it is. Back tyre, driver's side. Those little fucking shithead punks, who the hell do they think they're dealing with?

Sam's out now too.

SAM What is wrong with you? Have you gone crazy?

RICH Oh, now *he's* mad. *He's* upset.

You telling me you didn't hear it?

SAM Hear what?

RICH   You didn't hear it, just now?

SAM   What, your impression of Samuel L Jackson with
Tourette's Syndrome?

RICH   Before that. Earlier? When we were driving?

SAM   What are you talking about?

RICH   I'm talking about that.

And I point to it. He screws up his face. Looks like
he isn't gonna come round at first, then, in this huff,
he marches round the corner, fists balled at his sides.
Reminds me of Julia when she doesn't want to have a
bath, she does exactly the same thing. Yeah, that's right,
he reminds of a little girl.

He sees the tyre.

SAM   Oh great.

RICH   You didn't hear that?

SAM   No I did not hear that.

RICH   Well, that's why I stopped. Because I did hear it.

SAM   Bloody hoodlums.

RICH   Huh?

SAM   You got CAA?

RICH   Do I have CAA, this guy. What the hell do I do for a
living?

Don't be so fucking stupid Sam. I got a spare in the back.
And the tools.

SAM   Of course you do,

RICH   He says, like he's in some kind of sulk.

So I get out the jack, the tools, and go for the tyre but, oh fuck, fucking shit, my back. Ouch. God I landed hard back there.

SAM   You need a hand?

RICH   I'm fine, I tell him. But fuck is my back killing me. Gonna need some painkillers.

I set everything out on the boulevard and ease myself down, gently, beside the tyre and get on with it. Everything is more fucking difficult than it should be. I feel like Beth stabbed me in my spine. Pretty impressive, I'll give her that.

Then I hear this door slamming behind me in the distance. And this voice. Hey, it's saying. Rich? Sam? Is that you?

I try to turn my head round but – ouch – the back is not liking that. I strain my eyes. And this guy walks into view. Fucking great. It's –

SAM   Matthew Wheeler!

RICH   Says Sam, in this really weird voice. And then I realise, of course, fucking Matthew Wheeler. I've pulled over right in front of his house. Wasn't really thinking that one through, was I?

Sam, Jesus, I thought you were in England, he goes.

SAM   Yeah, well, I am. Not now, of course. Now I'm here. Just home for a…visit.

RICH   Uh huh, he goes, like he really gives a fuck. At least Sam didn't mention Dad, I'll give him that much. Then he's turning to me, Boy, that's sure some flat you got there,

Rich. Like I need him to tell me this. Then he goes, You need a hand?

And I want to shout, at both of them, No I do not need a goddam hand, what I need is to be left alone, and not have to worry about all this other shit.

Then I think, hang on here. Let's kill two birds.

So I go, Actually Matt, it would be great if Sam here could use your phone.

They both just look at me.

SAM   Why?

RICH   To call Mom. And tell her we're on our way. Here's the number of the hospital switchboard. The room is 0934.

SAM   Doesn't anyone have a mobile phone in this country?

RICH   Only the drug dealers, I say. And me and fucking Matthew Wheeler have a good laugh about that.

        You're welcome to use the phone if you like, Sam, says Wheeler.

        Then Sam kinda smiles, and goes:

SAM   Tell me if you don't want me to.

RICH   And there's this weird, like moment. Then Wheeler tells him it's all right, and they trot off to the house.

        'Bout fucking time. A little peace and quiet, that's all I need. Just a few minutes to myself.

        (*As he works.*) Fucking Matthew Wheeler. I mean, sure we hung out a bit in school, played hockey 'n' shit, had him over for parties at my house, whatever. Usual stuff. But this guy. He won't fucking drop off the face of the earth like everyone else. For one thing, he marries Cindy Baker right out of school. Yeah, I know – Cindy Baker. Maybe he knocked her up, I dunno. So they're hitched and the next thing he does is buy this house around the corner from his Mom's place, and of course he's still working at the Canadian Tire up the road there and even though I'm over in Mississauga at this point, with Beth, every single time I talk to Mom it's all about how fucking Matthew Wheeler got her a discount on fertilizer and how he keeps asking how me and Sam are doing. Mom thinks we should all get together for dinner. Thank God that never happened. Then last year I run into him at the car show, and we have to chit-chat and next thing you know it turns out that his little boy and Julia will be at school together and maybe they can play. Man, LEAVE ME ALONE. MOVE ON WITH YOUR LIFE. SCHOOL IS OVER.

Pause, as he continues to work.

'Tell me if you don't want me to.' What does *that* mean?

10

SAM   He begs for it. Which is a nice surprise. I don't even have to ask. Funny how people change, isn't it?

You see, we have this ongoing debate at work. Active. Passive. Bottom. Top. These terms. We throw them around, but really, what do they mean? They mean who fucks who. They mean who penetrates who, basically. But for whatever reason it doesn't sound right to say that, to say 'I'm a penetrator' or 'I'm the penetrated'. Instead we say these ridiculous euphemisms – and they aren't even helpful. Bottom? Top? That's just geography, easily changed, that doesn't tell you anything. Active? What is *that*? Do you show up in a sweatsuit and headphones? But the best, the absolute best, has to be passive. Like, what, you're just supposed to lie there half-dead, limp like some corpse, with not a care in the world? Maybe reading a magazine or doing the shopping list? As Liam says, No one would want to fuck someone truly passive. You might as well have a hole in the wall. Who'd want that?

I'll tell you who. Matthew Wheeler.

He was cute, I'll give him that – and he's still not bad. But he was so obvious. I mean, I could tell, that first time he came over for one of Rich's parties, the rest of his friends didn't even acknowledge I was there, and that was fine because, you know, I had mix tapes to make. But Matthew Wheeler, he comes right into my room, and leans against my door, beer in hand, and starts getting all chatty with me, turns out he likes Sarah McLaughlin too. I mean, *Sarah.* Not likes her, as in wants to fuck her, but likes her as in knows all the words to 'Hold On'. Weird for a jock, don't you think? I thought it weird. I also thought it weird when in the middle of the night I heard my door creak open, and this soft tiptoeing across the room. A weight on the bed beside me. A whisper.

Sam. It's just me. Matthew.

I'm excited. But I don't say anything.

Then there's this weight, on top of the blanket. Is it okay to sleep in your bed? The sofa is uncomfortable. Then there's this hand, underneath the blanket. And I'm thinking, well, I'm thinking thank you God, basically. And I go to roll over and face him. But there's this other hand, on my shoulder.

Just lie there, okay? he says. But tell me if you don't want me to.

And that's how it begins. Every couple of weeks, Matthew Wheeler finds some reason to sleep over at our place. And that sofa of ours never gets any more comfortable. I mean, whatever, I'm not complaining. When you're sixteen a regular shag is a regular shag. But still, it was a bit one-sided. No, it was totally one-sided. I was only supposed to say when I wanted him to stop. Which I didn't but, like, he could have at least made an effort. Could he at least let me do something back to him? No. That's not what he wanted. He wanted a hole in the wall. He wanted totally passive.

Well, I haven't been like that in a long time.

I wait until we get to the stairs before I grab him around the waist.

And here he is, begging for it. Funny how people change.

11

RICH How long does it take to make a phone call? I have changed the tyre, which is no easy thing I would like to say, but I do it, even with my back, in the time it takes him to go, call, and come back. And what does he come out with when he gets back outside?

SAM I couldn't get through.

RICH He couldn't… This guy.

What have you been doing then?

SAM   Catching up,

RICH   He says. Stupid grin on his face. Fucking Matthew
        Wheeler comes out of the front door.

        Everything okay now? he asks.

SAM   Just perfect,

RICH   Says Sam. And he's got this smile. What do *they* have to
        catch up on?

        Yeah, the back tyre's all fine now, I say.

SAM   It sure is.

RICH   Then Matthew's coming over to shake my hand, saying
        we should all have dinner again soon, Cindy would love
        to see us both, maybe bring Julia around. I kinda smile
        and nod, and then he's making his way back into the
        house.

        He doesn't say anything to Sam.

        Fucking Matthew Wheeler. Why the hell is he walking
        funny?

12

SAM   It's no coffee, but fucking Matthew Wheeler has
        definitely perked me up. As we head down Bellamy,
        on the new tyre, I see the cookie-cutter houses and the
        suburban continuum in a whole new light. Maybe those
        repressed people in those repressed little houses deserve
        their repressed little lives. Maybe they've been begging
        for it, just like our friend back there. Maybe this is where
        they deserve to be, in this zoo for the dull, this cage for

the mediocre. Maybe they're begging for it. (*He looks at RICH.*) Maybe.

We head down Bellamy and as I happen to turn my head to the left, the first happy sight of this depressing hamlet of Hell comes into view.

Hey, it's Indian Mound! I say.

RICH   Yeah,

SAM   He says. Glad to see kids still go sledding, I say. Thought it might have gone out of fashion.

RICH   No,

SAM   He says. You ever take Julia down here? I say.

RICH   Yeah,

SAM   He says. Then out of nowhere, he hits the breaks, flicks on his indicator and we skid – literally – across the slushy surface of Bellamy Road into the parking lot of Doughnut World.

RICH   Yes, she likes to come down here a lot,

SAM   He says, as he jerks up the emergency break, turns off the engine and opens the door. He starts surveying the collected kids speeding down Indian Mound.

Of course *I* don't expect to receive any information about what the fuck is going on. But fortunately I'm able to piece it together. I step out of the car and say, While you're looking to kidnap your own daughter, I'm going inside for a coffee and a doughnut, you want one?

RICH   Okay.

SAM   You still like bear claws?

RICH   Yes.

SAM   What would be amazing now is a Boston Cream, a double double, and a post-shag smoke. Then, as if reading my mind Rich goes,

RICH   You know you can't smoke in there.

SAM   Sorry?

RICH   You can't smoke in there.

SAM   Where?

RICH   Doughnut World.

SAM   I can't smoke in Doughnut World?

RICH   What did I just say?

SAM   It's Doughnut World.

RICH   Yeah well –

SAM   People go in there to smoke.

RICH   Not any more.

SAM   Why the fuck would they introduce such a stupid rule. No one's going to go here any more. Do people go here?

RICH   I don't know.

SAM   Because I bet they don't. Cigarette, coffee, doughnut. You can't have one without the other. They're going to go bankrupt.

RICH   It's not them. Doughnut World didn't decide, idiot. It's city-wide. No smoking. Anywhere.

SAM   What?

RICH   You didn't know?

SAM   You're shitting me.

RICH   Man, you really have been away a long time.

SAM   I mean, like, this is what I do not fucking need! Is nothing
       sacred? What kind of freakish puritanical backwater
       streak swept through this place while I've been gone? No
       smoking?

       I fumble around with the pack of fags, pull one out and
       light it. Of all the ridiculous… If I lean right against the
       wall I can kinda just block out the wind. Barely.

       I look over the snowdrifts packed up at the edges of
       the lot. Just over the road kids are tobogganing down
       Indian Mound. Look at him go, fucking fast down the hill
       and…oooh, nice jump off that, what is it, have they built
       a ramp there? It's nice to see there's still a little purity in
       childhood these days, nice that instead of video games
       and gang warfare some kids would prefer fresh air and
       speeding down a hill towards a home-made ramp. (*Pause.*)
       Not that it's really a hill. It's a mound. An Indian Mound.
       Quite literally, a mound of Indians. What's the story
       behind it again? I read it enough times. It's up there on
       the plaque, on that rock right at the very top. Some big
       battle between two tribes who used to live in harmony
       and then they just ripped into each other, tore each other
       apart.

       Ooh. Nice jump.

       Then they realised the madness of what they'd done
       and then they just built this huge mound and dumped
       in the bodies, burying them together. As one. Or some
       symbolic shit like that. Turned the place into a sacred
       burial ground and everything. And now we go sledding
       on their graves. Respectful.

What *are* those kids using as a ramp? They are getting some amazing height.

I exhale the smoke and watch it mix with the vapour of my breath. It's like blowing out exhaust – I remember walking to school, pretending to be a car. I remember sledding down this place here, Indian Mound, pretending to be a jet plane. For the first time in a long time, I remember…I remember home.

Is that ramp…is it moving?

13

RICH   (*Out of breath.*) This guy. My back is like fucking broken and he's yelling at me to,

SAM   Hurry up!

RICH   And, you know, it's not like the kid is going anywhere. And Sam's clearly going to get there first and I don't see, really, how me hurrying up is going to help the situation in the slightest. We're talking packed down snow here too. You know how it gets. All slippery and shit from the sleds going over it. And I am not falling on that. 'Cause there's no way I'll be getting back up.

The kids are looking at us like a pair of fucking freaks, and I'm sure that's exactly what we look like. Sam scrambling over there, screaming,

SAM   Get away from him you little bastards!

RICH   And me limping along in the back. Sam gets there and I see him drop down to his knees. Practically every kid on the hill is gathering round now to see what's going on. I push my way to the front.

Slumped down in the snow in front of Sam is this kid and he's not looking too good. White, white skin. Slightly blue lips. And eyes firmly closed.

SAM   Oh shit, oh shit. Everyone stand back I know CPR.

RICH   You do?

SAM   Yes, I have to for work!

RICH   And then he's in there undoing the kid's scarf and propping back his head, pinching his nose and giving him mouth to mouth. All the other kids are just standing around. I point to one with one of those court jester type hats on.

What the hell were you doing? You can't use him as a ramp!

Kid just looks at me.

Hey, I say, I'm talking to you!

Kid looks at his friends, side to side. Then says, He was just lying there. So we started jumping over him. He didn't seem to mind.

I'm about to give this twisted little fuck a quick lesson on morality when I hear:

SAM   (*Clutching his groin.*) Owwww!

RICH   And I look over and see Sam grabbing his crotch and rolling on the ground. The blue-lipped kid is now up on his knees and yelling, get off me you faggot! The mouth on this kid. What is he, like ten?

He jumps on Sam and is trying to get his hands round his neck, so I make a grab for him…which is fucking murder on my back. I get him by the hood of his coat and pull him backwards so he falls on his ass. Then it's easy. I hold him down with one hand.

Why are you talking to him like that? He's trying to save your life, I say.

He was trying to make out with me! he says.

SAM   Oh come on!

RICH   I look at the kid and say, He was not trying to make out with you. He was trying to help you. You were unconscious. You would have frozen to death. These little punks were using you as a ramp.

He looks at me like I'm speaking another language. Of course they were, he says. I let them.

You what? I say.

I let them, he says. It's fun. I can just lie there and I don't have to do anything.

This is too fucking weird. I look back and forth between them. Out of the corner of my eye, I see Sam is still rolling in the snow.

I point to Blue Lips. Thing one: you shouldn't let your friends treat you this way.

Court Jester pipes up. He's not my friend – he's my brother.

SAM   What the *fuck*?

RICH   Thing two: don't go hurting people who are trying to help.

SAM   Yeah!

RICH   Blue Lips looks at me and goes, Fuck off and die.

        I grab him tighter. And finally, thing three: do you know
        a little girl named Julia? About your age? She comes here
        to play sometimes?

        Then I hear this shout from Court Jester. Ew gross! These
        two are kiddie fiddlers! This one wants to bum-fuck
        my brother and this one wants to rape some little girl!
        Paedophiles! Paedophiles! He looks at Blue Lips, and
        they both start shouting it. Paedophiles! *Paedophiles!*

        Suddenly I'm aware we're attracting a lot of attention up
        and down the hill. So I look at *my* brother.

SAM   Can we just get the fuck out of here please?

RICH   For the first time since he stepped off that plane, Sam and
        I are in total agreement.

14

SAM   We're heading down Eglinton now and our in-depth
        analysis of the Twilight Zone experience we've just had
        on Indian Mound has gone like this.

        Me: Wow, that was fucked up, eh Rich?

        Rich:

RICH   Yeah.

        Pause.

SAM   That kid was –

RICH   I know.

       Pause.

SAM   And, God, his own brother it's just –

RICH   Yeah.

       Pause.

SAM   I guess I should say thanks for –

RICH   Don't mention it.

       Pause.

SAM   No, really, thanks for –

RICH   I said, don't mention it.

       Pause.

SAM   So, I decide to steer the conversation around to a subject closer to both our hearts.

       You see much of Matthew Wheeler these days?

RICH   Not if I can help it.

SAM   Oh?

RICH   Yeah.

SAM   You don't know how things are going with Cindy?

RICH   No idea.

SAM   Oh right. I thought you two would be close.

RICH   Well we're not.

SAM   I thought you'd want to relive your glory days.

RICH   No.

SAM   Catch up on old times.

RICH   No.

SAM   You probably have a lot in common, the kids, living here again, and –

RICH   We have fuck all in common, so drop it.

SAM   Well. Excuse me.

        We pull into the hospital car park, and circle the levels. He parks the car and turns the engine off. And we sit there.

        Should we…should we talk before we go up to see them?

RICH   Do we have to?

SAM   Oh, come on! Can you at least update me on what the doctors have been, you know, and how Mom is doing, and what I should…expect. Please. I'm very tired.

        And he sighs.

RICH   Fine. There's a Burger King in there. I'm kinda hungry anyway.

SAM   A Burger King. In a hospital. Does nobody else see the irony in this?

        We get in there, order, and the coffee tastes like piss but I'm sure it has caffeine in it, which is all that matters. The Whopper with cheese, large fries, and Minute Maid seems to have put Rich in a more talkative mood. I try to ease him into it.

        So, how's the boxing going?

RICH   Okay I guess. Don't get as much time on the bag as I'd
        like. Definitely don't get as much time at the club. But,
        you know, I do what I can. It's good for my health.

SAM   He says, as he licks some of the over-spilled burger
        grease off his fingers.

        Someone trying to beat the shit out of you is good for
        your health?

RICH   As a matter of fact, it is.

SAM   I choose not to point out that his stomach is spilling over
        onto the table.

RICH   And it's not just the physical work-out. It's good for your
        mental health. See, forget your *Raging Bull*, your *Million
        Dollar Baby*, your *Rocky*. It ain't about violence or success
        or following your fucking dreams. The best thing about
        boxing is…the silence.

SAM   The silence?

RICH   That's right. You get in a ring, it's just you and the other
        guy. You meet eyes. And you don't take your eyes off
        each other until the fight's done. In that time you've
        found out everything you need to know about him. How
        aggressive he is. How defensive. How predictable. How
        creative. How he deals with mistakes, how he deals with
        success. Is he a killer, or is he compassionate. Is he driven
        to win – or is he just looking for an excuse to fail. You
        get to find all that out – but you don't have to say one
        fucking word. You do it through moving. You do it all in
        silence.

SAM   I mean, this is really enlightening. Who knew my brother
        had such insights into the human condition? If it's that
        inspiring, he should get back to his boxing sometime.

I feel like I should say that last bit. You'll have to get back to it sometime then.

RICH   Yeah, well, it doesn't look like it's on the cards in the immediate future.

SAM   Yeah, about that. How…how're you doing now?

RICH   Back's sore. Fucking Beth. Fucking kids.

SAM   No, I mean generally. How are you? With all…this.

RICH   What, you mean Dad?

SAM   Sure.

RICH   I'm… I don't know. I still can't believe it. Last week he was fine. You know what he did last week?

SAM   What?

RICH   Shovelled the roof. Of the house. The *roof.* This is a sixty-five year old man we're talking about here. I pulled into the driveway and I was like, What the fuck are you doing? You'll break your neck. He got all serious on me, clenched his fists, you know that thing that he does? Then this smile cracks on his face. And he threw a snowball at me. And now? He looks so…feeble. He looks deflated. Last week he shovelled the roof. Now, we get excited if his eyes twitch.

SAM   He's still the same then?

RICH   It's not looking good.

SAM   You know, most people recover. From this GBS.

RICH   They do?

SAM   Yeah.

RICH   How do you know?

SAM   I know someone, in London, he / told me.

RICH   This Liam?

SAM   (*Surprised.*) Yes.

RICH   He your boyfriend?

SAM   (*Even more surprised.*) Ah…no. We just work together.

RICH   Oh okay. You mentioned him a lot. I kinda thought, you know.

SAM   Is he my boyfriend? What is *that* all about? As if every time I mention a guy I've got to be dating him…

        Well, he's a nurse, Rich.

RICH   I thought he worked with you.

SAM   He's a nursing *student*. So I've been quizzing him about Dad.

RICH   And what's he say?

SAM   Well, that it goes like this. You're fine, then suddenly, you get ill quickly, you know, the electrical wiring / in the house goes wrong.

RICH   Don't call it that!

SAM   Sorry, sorry, the nervous system, it goes all wrong. And suddenly, before you know it you're weak, and then you're paralysed. Then it takes you ages to recover. But you do recover. And that's why Liam told me not to think of the G, the B, and the S, as Guillain-Barré Syndrome. He said to think of it as Getting Better Slowly. Because that's what you have to do. You have to get better slowly.

RICH   He doesn't seem to be getting better at all.

SAM   Maybe you need to give it more time.

RICH   His condition hasn't changed.

SAM   It hasn't been that long. Maybe the slowly is, you know, really slow.

RICH   Maybe.

SAM   What have you told Julia?

RICH   I…I just told her her Grandpa was sick.

SAM   Do you think I'll get a chance to see her?

RICH   How long are you staying?

SAM   My ticket is for Monday.

RICH   Monday?

SAM   Yeah, I have to get back / to work.

RICH   You're only staying until Monday, are you kidding me?

SAM   No – I mean, if I need to stay I can always change the ticket, but I thought that I'd come and just make sure / everything's okay, in person.

RICH   I cannot believe you, you are something, you know that? You are fucking something!

SAM   What are you talking about?

RICH   You don't get to be a tourist in our lives, Sam.

SAM   A tourist? What?

RICH   You don't get to parachute in and hug Mom and see Dad and make everything right. That's not how it works. Do you have any idea how hard this has been for me?

SAM   Oh cry me a river, Rich. I didn't even find out until Tuesday, I got here as fast as I could!

RICH   And you're leaving as fast as you can too!

SAM   I have to work!

RICH   Yeah, wouldn't want to lose that precious bar job.

SAM   Oh, fuck you!

RICH   You know, I've seen you looking at me since I picked you up at the airport. I've seen you after we left Beth's, that worried look all over your face. Every time you looked at me in the car. Worry. You think I've fucked up my life.

SAM   No –

RICH   You think I've fucked it all up and I'm gonna be stuck here, stuck in the past for ever, just like fucking Matthew Wheeler. Well let me tell you something. Things haven't turned out the way I hoped they would. And, yeah, okay, sure, I've now got an ex-wife, and I'm a single father, and I'm living with my parents again, and I'm running around stressed out of my mind trying to make ends meet, and it goes round and round, just stuck in this rut. And now I'm looking after Mom trying to keep her from losing it, and talking about I don't even know what with doctors, and having to say 'Grandpa's really sick', those words, how can I say those words?

SAM   Rich –

RICH   And all this is hard Sam, really really hard. But I do it. I do it, and what I do *not* do is fuck off to another country, to have some extended party, doing whatever I want, thinking only about myself. I do not do that. I stay here, and I live with being stuck in the rut, and try little by little…to get better. I try to get better slowly. And it's not easy. But that's what responsibility is all about, Sam. That's what makes you a man. But I don't expect you to know about that. Because you never have. And why would you change?

SAM   And with that he stuffs his last fry in his mouth and walks out of Burger King. I want to shout at him, call him a fat fucker, tell him he doesn't know me, that he's never known me and how dare he, how the fuck dare he presume to pass judgement on me, how dare he take out his shit on me because that is not what I am here for, that is not why I am here.

This is what I want to shout. But I don't. I am so tired. And, you know, once the tears start, it's hard to stop them.

15

RICH   Out the door. Left. Card shop. Chapel. Left. Offices. Stairwell – no fuck *that*. Ah, black line on floor. Double doors. Follow black line. Turn right. And, here we go. Elevators.

Button. Wait. Tap foot.

Fucking Sam.

Bing. Doors. In. Press eight. Shut. (God these are big.)

Floor one. Two. Three. Stop. Doors. Nurse with vials. Of blood. Polite smile. Presses six. Six? Can't he just walk? Doors. Fourth floor, fifth, sixth, and surprise, stop. Doors. Him out, walking quickly. Doors. Seven. And eight. Doors.

Walk out. Turn left, quick right. Lounge. Television. Left. Doors. Long hallway. Phone. Pick it up.

Rings. Again. Nurse answers. Say who I am. Tells me to hold on. Wait. Wait. God, they do love to make you wait. Wait. Comes back on. Okay, you can come in now. Remember to disinfect your hands. Hangs up.

Disinfect my…of course I'm going to disinfect my… Fucking nurse.

Container on wall. Pump. Clear liquid. Hate that smell. Gotta remember not to rub my eyes.

Through doors. Left. Short hallway. More doors. ICU.

Walk slowly now. Hear the sounds of beeps and whirs. Machines. Whispers. See the nurse at the desk. The one with the brown hair. Ass a bit big, but I'd still fuck her. She looks up. Motions over to Dad's bed with an 'it's okay to go over' look. Thanks for your permission.

And there's Mom. In the chair beside the bed. Holding Dad's hand, she half turns, sees me, smiles. Then she creases her eyebrows. Mouths it. Where's Sam? I go over.

Bathroom, I say. He'll be right up.

Mom pats my shoulder. And we sit there. Looking at Dad.

If I'm totally honest, I hate this fucking place. First off, it's so quiet you can barely keep awake more than five minutes. Secondly, where is the fucking dignity for these people? I mean, over there, classic example. There's some old guy, machines all over his face, and his little hospital gown thing hitched so far up half his dick is hanging out. Why is that necessary? Can't some nurse just cover him up? Isn't that what they're paid for?

Apparently not. Apparently they're paid to write things down on clipboards and to tell you to disinfect your hands. And there's no TV in here or anything. So what're you gonna do? Read? Come on.

I see the nurse pick up the phone. Looks over at us. Says something back and hangs up. Here we go. Mom sees me looking, and turns her head to the door.

There's like this waiting now, this anticipation. And I know he's just doing it for effect. And the fucker, it's working. 'Cause Mom and I are both staring, sitting there, just waiting and waiting.

And then, finally, all meek and mild, he strolls into the ICU. You can practically hear the angelic choir, you know? See the golden light shine down on him. Sam, the perfect one, has arrived. Gives us a little wave.

Mom can barely contain herself, puts Dad's hand back on the bed and gets up. He's coming over now and they meet up halfway, big hugs and lots of sobbing into his chest. He's looking a bit teary-eyed himself. Typical.

The hug goes on forever, and they go through all the usual forms. You know, first it's the grip-you-really-tightly hug. Then it moves on to the rubbing-your-hands-up-and-down-each-other's-back-while-you-say-things hug. Then you've got the slightly-rocking-from-side-to-side-hug, followed by the grip-relaxing-and-the-let-me-have-a-look-at-you kind of hug. The whole time the nurse is watching, this kind of sour look. She catches my eye, looks back to Sam and Mom and then tries to say something to me with her eyes. But she's across the room and I can't make out what the fuck she's getting at. So she pushes back her chair and tiptoes over to me.

You're only really supposed to have two visitors at a time, she says.

Well, my brother just got in from England, I say.

Still, it's policy. And it's not really fair to the other patients, she says.

Not really fair? These people don't care, they're all half fucking unconscious. Is it policy for them to have their cocks on display? I don't think so. I don't say this of course. Instead I just kind of look at her and go, Yeah, all right I'll step outside.

But then Mom's like, No no no Richard, you and your brother stay here. Your father will be so happy to have his two sons visiting him together. It will mean so much to him. And besides, she whispers, I really need a piddle.

SAM   Mom!

RICH   Which only encourages her.

Well I do, she's saying. It's that damn tea in the cafeteria downstairs. It makes me all pissy, ask your brother.

And Sam turns to me as if I'm supposed to confirm the whole fucking thing.

It's like, can we please not talk about Mom's urine? Come on.

Thankfully, Mom kisses Sam on the cheek and scurries out of the room saying she'll be back in fifteen minutes. The nurse looks pleased. And goes back to her clipboard.

So. Sam looks at me. I look at him. And then his eyes kinda dart down to Dad lying there. But only for a second. He looks back at me. And he's about to say something, so I jump in.

                You should rub his hand.

SAM   I – what?

RICH   You should take his hand and rub it.

SAM   Dad was never really a hand-holding kind of guy.

RICH   Yeah I know that but they say it might help.

SAM   How?

RICH   It might get the nerves going, you know? He might be
         able to feel it.

SAM   Oh.

RICH   He looks a little bit unsure as he edges along the bed. He
         reaches out to take Dad's hand and kinda pauses.

         You just pick his hand up.

SAM   Yeah but the tubes and things, I don't want to…

RICH   This guy. I go around the other side of Dad and take that
         hand.

         See? You just pick it up. And rub it. Like this. You just
         stay away from the tubes and shit.

SAM   It feels so…heavy.

RICH   Yeah.

SAM   He looks so small.

RICH   I know.

SAM   And the colour of his skin is…why is it swollen here?

RICH   The fluid collects.

SAM   Oh.

RICH   Keep rubbing.

        A pause, while they both rub the hands.

SAM   So can he feel this?

RICH   They don't know. But in case he can it's kind of like why
        not, you know? It's the same thing with talking to him.

SAM   What do you mean?

RICH   We're supposed to talk to him. In case he can hear us.

SAM   In case he can hear us? You mean there's a chance he's
        conscious?

RICH   What, I thought nurse Liam told you everything you
        needed to know about GBS.

SAM   Oh, don't be such an ass–

RICH   The doctors did some tests and he's got brain activity.
        Means he might be able to hear us. Means he might
        know what's going on. Only problem is he's, you know…

SAM   He's trapped in there.

RICH   Yeah.

SAM   Fucking hell.

RICH   Yeah.

        Pause.

SAM   You know that was a shitty thing to say to me down there
        in Burger King,

RICH   He says. And I'm thinking, Only you Sam. So I say, Only
        you Sam.

SAM   Only me what?

RICH   Only you could be standing there looking at your Dad in some serious medical, you know, and you're thinking about you. How I hurt your little feelings.

SAM   Yeah well maybe seriously upsetting me right before I have to come in and be supportive to Mom, before I have to come in and see Dad looking like, God, *this*; maybe pulling some macho self-righteous bullshit on me is not that best way for you to help me help the situation.

RICH   All I do is tell it like it is.

SAM   You tell it like it is?

RICH   That's right.

SAM   Do you now?

RICH   Yes.

SAM   How can you tell it like it is when you know this much, this much about me.

RICH   Yeah, well, and if that's true then why? Why do I know that much about you?

SAM   Because you've never wanted to know.

RICH   Because I can't find anything out when you run away.

SAM   I didn't run away. I moved away, okay?

RICH   Moved, ran, call it what you want. It was your choice to get as far away from us as you could.

SAM   Not away from you. Away from this place.

RICH   You couldn't move downtown?

SAM   It's not the same.

RICH   Yeah, that's right. It's a lot harder to hide who you are when you're downtown – much better if you're on the other side of the fucking ocean!

SAM   I'm not hiding. I'm not… Okay, what the fuck is this about? You never had any issue with me being in London before. What's going on here?

RICH   What's going on is you not being here for your family.

SAM   So what are you saying, you want me to be here?

RICH   It would just be nice if –

SAM   You want me to be here because you *need* my help?

RICH   I don't…

        This guy. Who the fuck does he think he is? I need his help? I *need* it? What a load of…

SAM   Well?

RICH   And I'm about to tell him. I'm about to fucking, to fucking lay it on the line for the last time with this guy, to just, to just. And I'm just about to…

        But before I can even open my mouth there's a tapping on the shoulder. It's the nurse.

        Excuse me, she says. Your mother wants both of you to come outside to the waiting area. I clamp my jaw and feel my shoulders go tense.

        I look at the nurse, trying to decide if she's bullshitting me or not. And I'm thinking…big ass. But I'd still fuck her.

16

SAM   If I have to deal with any more shit today I am *actually* going to stab out my own eye with the nearest sharp object. First we're rushing to the hospital, then we're stopping at every fucking imaginable place along the way. First Mom wants us in the ICU, then two seconds later we're being called out again. I mean.

When we get out into the corridor it's like, *fuck*. Let me paint the scene for you. You've got Mom, Beth, and then this little girl who I know, on a logical level, must be Julia, but seeing her it just like doesn't compute. I see them all standing there and I'm like whoa, where's the hidden cameras? And I can feel Rich is like very whoa because I'm sure he reckons Beth might be here to finish him off. But then Julia is like, Daddy! And then she comes out with it: Uncle Sam!

She runs up to me and I duck down in time to get this big hug and it feels…great. She doesn't let go, and it starts feeling better than great. It feels…it feels like something I need. Like something I've been missing.

But let me tell you this: nothing makes you feel older than how much children grow in your absence. Look at her. I mean she's big. She's like a little person. She's dressed better than me for God's sake. Okay, slight exaggeration, this shirt was fifty quid. She's dressed better than…Rich. Not saying much, but for an eight year old she's looking pretty amazing.

I stand up and suddenly re-enter the world of the adults. You know, four people standing around in some serious tension, but have to keep the illusion of friendliness going for the sake of a child who, by the way, knows full well exactly what's going on. But we all pretend nevertheless because that's the way stupid repressed people treat children.

RICH   Oh look Sam. It's Beth,

SAM   Says Rich.

Hi again, I say.

Mom's face is so splotched with red and streaked in tears it's hard to recognise her. It must be a lot for her. All of us in one place. She starts speaking, so quietly it's hard to hear her. Says she came out of the ICU and there were Beth and Julia coming down the hall. Isn't it a nice surprise?

Beth's standing with her arms folded. She just looks at Rich and goes, I thought I'd bring Julia.

RICH   Oh,

SAM   He says.

To see Sam, she says.

RICH   Oh.

SAM   And then Mom is chiming in with, Oh isn't that lovely, isn't it great to see your Uncle Sam, Julia? And she's off in floods of tears again and excusing herself as she jogs away. And I'm pretty sure we can all hear the word 'piddle' echoing down the hall behind her.

17

RICH   She keeps asking me if she can see her Grandpa.

No, I tell her, you don't want to honey.

Yes I do, she says.

It's not nice, I say. It might be scary for you to see him.

She kinda shrugs and looks around at Beth, as if she might get a better answer from her mother. Knowing fucking Beth, that's not such a insane idea, anything to contradict me. Julia whips round again to look at me and her eyes say she's just had an idea.

Sometimes it's even scarier not to see, she says. Because you imagine. I think it's better to see, to know for yourself.

What am I supposed to say to that? It suddenly occurs to me it's better to just remove her from the whole situation. But this kid, it's like she can fucking read my mind, she knows me so well. Before I can even say anything, before I can even finish the thought she jumps up on me and wraps her legs around my thighs. Dad, she says, I want to go in!

Arrrg! My fucking back! I don't say that, of course. But my face says it all and I can see Beth give this little satisfied grin. I slide Julia's hands off my waist, and let her attach herself to my leg. A compromise.

SAM   What are you doing?

RICH   I look at him.

It's a bit difficult to pick her up at the moment.

Beth gives this chuckle. Again, I ignore.

Look, I say, we better get going.

SAM   Really?

RICH   Yeah, well, I don't think this is best place for…someone.

SAM   Oh.

RICH   And Beth goes, What? Why?

She wants to go in the ICU.

SAM   Ah.

RICH   And Beth says, I don't see anything wrong with that.

SAM   I don't know if that's such a good idea,

RICH   Says Sam. And I'm thinking, Okay Sam, thank you very much for backing me up here.

SAM   It could be…a bit disturbing.

RICH   And then Julia says, You think so Uncle Sam?

SAM   I think so honey.

RICH   Weirdly, this seems to be all that's needed. Julia looks at me and goes, Okay then.

I pat her on her head and say, You'll see him soon. We're gonna go now.

I look at Sam. And I'm thinking, let's kill two birds here. I go, You gonna stay here with Mom, then? But he just looks at me with these deep, dark-ringed eyes, as if to say:

SAM   Please God just let me have some sleep.

RICH   Julia saves him first. She's tugging at my sleeve going, *Dad.* Mom brought me here so I could see Uncle Sam. So either we all get to stay, or we all have to leave.

This kid.

18

SAM   G. B. S. The doctor says. Really slow. Like I'm some kind of idiot. And I want to say, I know the fucking alphabet, you asshole. Okay? I know the letters, Hell, I even know what they mean. I'm *not* my fucking brother. I am totally different. I can pronounce Guillain-Barré Syndrome, okay? I know what that is and what is does, what it is *doing* to my father. I know it's an unexplained illness. I know they think GBS has something to do with the body's immune system attacking itself. I know that it usually follows a period of sickness, a flu or infection or something. But I also know that most people get better slowly. I have a friend who has explained it to me. I say this last bit: I have a friend who explained it to me.

The doctor looks at me and nods. His look says, I have just enough time to look sympathetic, but I'm actually very busy. I mean…fuck *off* then.

We were almost out the door of the hospital when Mom came running down the hall with this guy in tow. I have no fucking idea why she felt it necessary for me to meet this man. I mean, what, am I supposed to approve of him? Am I supposed to feel reassured because I've met the doctor?

He obviously feels he has a duty to keep talking. It can be a very confusing and frustrating illness, he says. And then he looks right at me, and I swear to God, he goes, It's often helpful for relatives of a victim to think of the body's nervous system like the electrical wiring in a house…

And I cannot believe he is saying this to me, I cannot believe he's giving me this, and I just want grab him by the coat and shake him and say, It's nothing, nothing like the electrical wiring / in a house because a human, a person…

RICH   (*Simultaneous – speaking to 'the doctor'.*) It's got nothing to do with the electrical wiring in a house. You know why? Because if the electrical wiring goes wrong in *my* house, *I* know how to fix it. And if I don't, if I can't, I call the electrician, the expert, who comes around immediately and does it for me. So the question is –

SAM   And now Rich gets right up close to him.

RICH   Aren't you the expert? Aren't you the electrician? You're the one with the white coat and the brochures and the letters after your name. So tell me: why isn't the electricity back on?

SAM   The doctor isn't looking so sympathetic now. In fact, he's looking like he might say something quite un-sympathetic which, I feel, I should probably warn him against, knowing Rich as I do…although I really can't be fucked at the moment.

RICH   This isn't a house we're talking about. This is my father.

SAM   And with that Rich turns, and marches out of the hospital. It seems that even the sliding doors open extra fast in an attempt to get out of his way.

I look at the doctor. I should do a little damage control.

Sorry about my brother, I say. (*Pause.*) But to tell the truth, you are a little bit of a penis.

And, yes, I did say that last bit. Fuck damage control.

19

RICH   Me, Sam, and Julia get to the car and make our way out of the parking lot. Just under the hour, and yes I'll keep my two dollars, thank you very much you parking lot pricks. We pull out onto Lawrence and we're away. Julia's not happy. In the rear-view mirror I can see her scowling, her fists all balled up at her sides. I'll give Sam credit, though, he's doing his best to cheer her up.

SAM   The money is called pounds and pence. Or you can call a pound a quid. Like how you call a dollar a buck. Here. Check this out. This is a pound coin. And this is a two pound coin. Like a twoony. But worth more.

RICH   Then he reaches into his wallet and hands a small fat golden coin to her. I can see the smile crack across her face. Okay, I'm thinking, well done Sam.

It dawns on me that Sam doesn't really have any idea how smart this litle girl is. Showing her coins and shiny stuff is good for now, but in a few minutes she'll be drilling him with questions he never expected. I decide a pre-emptive attack is best. I point to a car out the window, ask her what it is.

Mustang GTS, she gets it first time.

Point to another one.

Yes, absolutely right, Mazda MVP.

Is this kid something or what? I look at Sam. He looks impressed.

SAM   I'm impressed.

RICH   When she gets a bit older, I say, I'm gonna show her some basics of auto mechanics. Don't want her to be some typical girl who can't look after herself.

SAM   You know, not all girls are –

RICH   He starts, like he's some kind of fucking feminist or something. So I cut the pussy off.

I make sure to tell her directions whenever we're going anywhere too, so she's not always getting lost like chicks do. Tell your Uncle Sam about the streets you know.

She doesn't need any more encouragement than that. Suddenly she's off. She tells him we've just turned back onto the 401 and that we're heading towards the DVP. And that the 401 will eventually take you out of the city and to the airport, and out and beyond into the whole big world. And the DVP will take you deep into the heart of the city, under bridges and through tunnels, until the roads get so narrow and the traffic gets so dense you don't move at all. The 401 and the DVP. They intersect here but they don't merge again, she says.

Isn't she amazing?

SAM   (*Falling asleep.*) She's amazing.

RICH   I see it's all beginning to catch up with Sam. It gets all quiet in the car. And I head down the 401, looking for the DVP.

20

SAM   There's a tugging at my trouser leg and when I come
       around I'm totally disoriented 'cause there's this little
       person right beside me. Then my eyes clear and I finally
       figure out where the fuck I am.

       Where I am is the driveway of 42 Bengrove Crescent
       – AKA home. Christ.

       Come in and lie down, says Julia.

       And I kind of stagger up and see Rich already at the front
       door with my bags. Julia has me by the hand now and
       takes me inside, chattering away about the cost of gas, of
       all things. I mean Rich is seriously starting to fuck up this
       little girl's brain. Mazda MVP? Mustang GTS? What the
       fuck? First thing tomorrow I'm showing this girl how to
       play with dolls. Okay? We're having a fucking tea party.
       We're going to play MASH. We're getting some My Little
       Pony up in this shit, all right?

       I step through the front door and the familiarity of home
       hits me like the inevitable blast of dried ice when they
       play 'SOS' at work. It's amazing how the place hasn't
       changed. There's the antique spinning wheel that nobody
       really knows why we have. The mat for Millie, the dog,
       still at the front door – even though she died like nine
       years ago. And of course, the specially commissioned
       poetry, engraved on the finest piece of lacquered tree
       bark, announcing your arrival into a house of high
       refinement. Would you like to hear it? It goes like this:

       There once was a house in Toronna'
       Where William lived with his wife Donna
       Rich was his first brat

Sam came after that
But by then Billy's hair was all gonna.

Truly a masterpiece of world literature.

RICH   You're in your old room,

SAM   Says Rich. And I shuffle to what was once a haven for me
        in the back corner of the house – my room. Still with a
        single bed, I see, and my Speech Arts trophy from Grade
        Six. I hear a clunking sound behind me.

RICH   Here's your suitcase.

SAM   Thanks.

        Pause.

RICH   Julia was very excited to see you.

SAM   She's so…big.

RICH   She's sad you're leaving so soon. She was saying in the
        car she doesn't want you to go on Monday.

SAM   Oh the guilt, the *guilt.* This fucking brother of mine, will
        he ever let up? Bed is just three feet away, I'm so, so
        close. If I could only just edge onto it, for even an hour,
        I could recharge, regain my abilities and deal with this
        unending onslaught of…guilt. But I can't. He won't give
        me a second to breathe.

        Rich, I just can't, I say. I have to get back.

RICH   Fine. I just hope you can explain whatever this pressing
        reason is to an eight-year-old girl.

SAM   And I have just about fucking had it with his shit. I can
        feel my back go all tense and my fists clench so tight my
        fingers feel they might come out the other sides of my
        hands. And seeing this, what does he have the nerve,

what does he have the *gall* to do? He smirks at me. I am ready to lose it.

What? What is so goddam funny?

RICH   You know who you look like when you do that? You know who you remind me of?

SAM   Yes I know.

RICH   So grow up then.

SAM   Grow up? What the hell are you talking about?

RICH   Oh you don't even know. Look at you, you're the spitting image –

SAM   Yeah, I know, who does it, it's –

RICH   The absolute spitting image of Julia.

SAM   (*Simultaneous with 'Julia'.*) Dad.

        Pause.

RICH   (*Quietly.*) Dad?

SAM   He did it all the time.

RICH   She does it as well. All the time…

        RICH begins to break down. He begins sobbing. It should be a protracted, ugly, and embarrassing release of emotion. At one point SAM may attempt to comfort him – RICH pushes him away. Eventually RICH regains his composure.

        Sorry.

SAM   It's okay Rich, I'm sure you needed –

RICH   Look, I'm only gonna ask you this one last time. Stay longer. Please. He's gonna get better. But he's gonna get better slowly. And it's gonna take longer, so it would be good if you could, it would mean a lot if you could just, I want... Just stay.

Pause.

SAM   I can't.

Pause.

I –

RICH   Okay. Fine. Okay then. Get some sleep. You look like you need it.

SAM   And with that, he walks out and pulls the door behind him.

I'm finally alone. But I don't want to be alone. Not right now. I need to speak to him, I need to hear his voice, even if I can't see him till Monday. (*He gets out his mobile phone.*) I don't care how much it's gonna cost, I need to...oh fuck, oh *shit* what is the dialling code from here, Jesus, what the hell is...yes, that's right.

011 44 7752 672911.

All these numbers. All these fucking...

Hello? Liam...it's me.

21

RICH   All I could find in the medicine cabinet were some Tylenol-3s left over from when I dislocated my shoulder playing hockey – the expiry date was fourteen years ago, but come on. As if these fucking things actually go off.

Then again, maybe they do, what the fuck do I know? Those things did nothing to make me more comfortable – I had the worst sleep ever. Every way I turned it felt like my spine was going to shoot through my chest. So when I heard the footsteps over my head at about five, I thought, What the fuck, why not? and got up.

As I come up the stairs I see Sam in the kitchen reading *The Sun.*

SAM   Hey.

RICH   Hey.

SAM   I didn't wake you up, did I?

RICH   Nah.

SAM   I didn't mean to sleep that long. I didn't mean to sleep through the night.

RICH   Don't worry about it. You didn't miss much. We just went and got Mom from the hospital.

SAM   Any news?

RICH   Nah. Still the same. They're running some tests, will let us know if they find anything out.

SAM   Haven't they been saying that for like days now?

RICH   Yes.

SAM   Do they know what they're doing over there?

RICH   I dunno. Just got to trust 'em I guess. Not like we know any better, do we?

SAM   No. We don't.

        Slight pause.

RICH   (*Indicating the paper.*) Fucking city's going to Hell.

SAM   Oh yeah?

RICH   Yeah. Every day it's murders and gangs and rapes.

SAM   Every city's got that, Rich.

RICH   I'm telling you, this place has changed.

SAM   It hasn't changed that much. Only difference I notice is that people *think* things are worse here, but they're not. Not really. People focus on the negative, but in other cities, they don't dwell so much.

RICH   Like London?

SAM   Like London.

        Slight pause.

RICH   I picked this up from the hospital gift shop last night. (*He hands SAM a card.*) Thought you could use it.

SAM   A phonecard?

RICH   Yeah. I asked them which got the best rates to the UK.

SAM   Well…thanks.

RICH   It's just that I don't want you jacking up the phone bill here with long distance calls. This way if you need to make calls, they'll be cheap.

SAM   (*Reading the back of the card.*) 'Simply dial 416-282-5574 then enter the fifteen number PIN code on the front of this card. Then dial the number you wish to call, including country code.' Simple.

RICH   It gets you pretty good rates, I just thought…you know.

SAM   I won't need to make many calls. But thanks.

RICH   Well, you know, if you don't, you can always leave it
       behind.

SAM   Then you'd have no excuse. You can use it to call me.

RICH   Julia would like that.

SAM   I would like that too.

RICH   When I was buying that phonecard, in the gift shop? Julia
       wanted to get you something as well.

SAM   Oh?

RICH   She'll kill me for giving it to you, but it's just too good.
       Here.

       *RICH holds up a candy bracelet. SAM holds out his hand.
       RICH puts it on SAM's wrist. A pause.*

       Anyway, look, the phonecard's here if you want it.

       And again he looks at me and goes,

SAM   I really don't need to use it. I mean look at all those
       numbers. There's nobody I need to call that badly.

RICH   There's nobody he needs to call?

       This guy.

Epilogue

RICH   Numbers.

SAM   Letters.

RICH   So many numbers.

SAM   Acronyms.

RICH   What do they tell you?

SAM   What do they really mean?

RICH   Numbers can tell you we waited twenty-six days to
         decide about life support.

SAM   G. B. S.

RICH   Numbers can tell you Dad had to be defibrillated four
         times.

SAM   What do those letters mean?

RICH   Numbers can tell you Sam flew back only once more.

SAM   George Bernard Shaw?

RICH   Numbers can tell you the suit he had to buy here cost
         four hundred and fifty bucks.

SAM   Guillain-Barré Syndrome?

RICH   Numbers can tell you it took us four hours to convince
         Mom he had no quality of life.

SAM   Getting Better Slowly?

RICH   Numbers can tell you time of death was 10:23.

SAM   That's what I'd like to think.

RICH   There are too many numbers. And they don't tell you a
         thing.

SAM   Sometimes you get better slowly.

RICH   (*To SAM.*) And sometimes you don't.

         Blackout.

Acknowledgements

First and foremost thank you to everyone in my family – Halls, Jardines, and Ilkays – for your endless love and encouragement. Thank you to the team behind the Toronto production of *GBS* for allowing me to begin this journey and to my agent, Nick Quinn, for helping me see it through. Many thanks to everyone in London who kindly read and advised on earlier versions of the play, especially Maria Aberg, Pia Furtado, Paul Higgins, Ruth Little and Simon Stephens. And thank you to Christopher Poulton for, well, everything.

Finally, a very special thank you to Hilary – you were there when I could not be, and you spoke when I was unable to, and for that I will always be grateful.